The Nature of Colour

A consideration of the perception of colour, the location of colour and the nature of the unperceived world

Thomas Green

123 Books

Copyright © 2011 by Thomas Green

All rights reserved. This book, or parts thereof, may not be reproduced in any form without permission.

A catalogue record for this book is available from the British Library

ISBN: 978-1-907962-02-8

Published by 123 Books

Reading, England

For Debbie

Contents

Preface 7

Introduction 9

1 At t_2 the cup-gap was wholly devoid of colour 13

2 At t_2 the cup-gap was coloured the same colour as the colour which I perceived at t_1 and t_3 (green) 23

3 At t_2 the cup-gap was coloured a particular but different colour to the colour which I perceived at t_1 and t_3 31

4 At t_2 the cup-gap was coloured but it wasn't a particular colour 37

5 Summary 45

6 Reasons to Favour the 'Infinite Manifold' View 49

Preface

The phenomenon of colour is very interesting and very important. I will take it for granted that you understand what I mean by the word 'colour'. When I go into the garden I perceive a tomato; this tomato has a particular shape and it has a particular colour – a particular shade of 'redness'.

Unfortunately, some people purport to be talking about colour when they are actually only talking about 'light waves which are themselves not coloured', or 'properties of objects which are themselves not coloured'. I will simply be using the word 'colour' to refer to the phenomenon of colour.

Colour is so important because the nature of the phenomenon provides great insight into the nature of the world, and it is the world which brought the human species into existence. Is the unperceived world pervaded with a plethora of colours? If so, it could also be pervaded with many other qualitative qualities; qualities such as those we refer to as 'pain' and 'elation'. Or, is the unperceived world wholly devoid of qualitative qualities? If so, the human species is seemingly very different to the world which evolved it.

Introduction

The subject of this book is the phenomenon of colour. In particular, our concern is to consider the relationship that exists between a perceiver of colour and the unperceived world that surrounds that perceiver. The *central question* which is to be addressed is: Does the unperceived world contain colour?

Let us consider the following scenario. At a particular time, t_1, I visually perceive a cup that appears to be coloured and located about one metre in front of me; if describing the colour I would call it green. A moment later at t_2 I close my eyes and am unable to see the cup. A moment later at t_3 I open my eyes and

The Nature of Colour

I again see a cup that appears to be exactly the same colour as before; let us assume that this is so. This scenario raises the following question: *At t_2 was the cup coloured or was it wholly devoid of colour?*

This question requires a little refinement, for at t_1 and t_3 whilst *the cup* appears to be green to me this could be due to the properties of *the gap* between me and the cup. Our central question is whether the unperceived world contains colour so we need to consider whether the unperceived world contains colours in either objects or in the gaps between objects. The term 'cup-gap' will be used to refer to the area of the world outside of me that includes both the cup and the gap between me and the cup. So, in order to address our central question

Introduction

the following question will be addressed: *At t_2 was the cup-gap coloured or was it wholly devoid of colour?* There are four possible answers to this question:

1   At t_2 the cup-gap was wholly devoid of colour.

2   At t_2 the cup-gap was coloured the same colour as the colour which I perceived at t_1 and t_3 (green).

3   At t_2 the cup-gap was coloured a particular but different colour to the colour which I perceived at t_1 and t_3.

4   At t_2 the cup-gap was coloured but it wasn't a particular colour.

These four possibilities will be considered in the first four chapters of the book. In *Chapter Five* I provide a summary of the first four chapters. Finally, in *Chapter Six* I provide some reasons why I believe one particular view to be the most accurate description of the world.

Chapter 1

At t_2 the cup-gap was wholly devoid of colour

Let us refer to the view that at t_2 the cup-gap is wholly devoid of colour as 'dispositionalism'. According to this view at t_2 the cup-gap simply contains the power or disposition to appear green when perceived. One of the first advocates of this view is Galileo who asserted:

> I think that tastes, odors, colors and so on are no more than mere names so far as the object in which we place them is concerned, and

that they reside only in the consciousness. Hence if the living creatures were removed, all these qualities would be wiped away and annihilated.[1]

Other notable advocates of this view are typically taken to be Robert Boyle, Descartes and John Locke; it is Locke who provides the fullest elucidation of the view. He argues that the unperceived world contains *Primary Qualities* and that the particular arrangements of these *Primary Qualities* give rise to certain powers – *Secondary Qualities*.

---

[1] Galileo, cited in Evan Thompson, *Colour Vision*, London: Routledge, 1995, p. 19.

These powers are located in objects and they cause particular colours to be seen when perceived. So, when a perceiver perceives a particular arrangement of wholly uncoloured *Primary Qualities* then they will perceive a particular colour. In Locke's words:

> Qualities thus considered in Bodies are, First such as are utterly inseparable from the Body, in what estate soever it be; such as in all the alterations and changes it suffers, all the force can be used upon it, it constantly keeps; and such as Sense constantly finds in every particle of Matter, which has the bulk enough to be perceived, and the Mind finds

inseparable from every particle of Matter, though less than to make itself singly be perceived by our Senses… These I call *original* or *primary Qualities* of Body, which I think we may observe to produce simple ideas in us, *viz.* Solidity, Extension, Figure, Motion, or Rest, and Number.

2dly, Such *Qualities*, which in truth are nothing in the Objects themselves, but Powers to produce various Sensations in us by their *primary qualities, i.e.* by the Bulk, Figure, Texture, and Motion of their insensible parts, as Colours, Sounds, Tastes, *etc*. These I call *secondary Qualities*.[2]

The *Ideas of primary Qualities* of Bodies *are Resemblances* of them, and their Patterns do really exist in the Bodies themselves; but the *Ideas, produced* in us *by* these *Secondary Qualities, have no resemblance* of them at all.[3]

---

[2] John Locke, *An Essay Concerning Human Understanding*, ed. P. H. Nidditch, Oxford: Oxford University Press, (1690/1975), %9-10.

[3] John Locke, *An Essay Concerning Human Understanding*, ed. P. H. Nidditch, Oxford: Oxford University Press, (1690/1975), VIII: %15.

The Nature of Colour

Another notable advocate of this position is Isaac Newton who established that light consists of rays that differ in refrangibility – the degree to which they are bent. He theorised that the colour of the cup that I perceive results from the way the cup differentially reflects these light rays. His experiments led him to claim that:

> The homogeneal Light and Rays which appear red, or rather make Objects appear so, I call Rubrifick or Red-making...the Rays to speak properly are not coloured. In them there is nothing else than a certain Power and

Disposition to stir up a Sensation of this or that Colour.[4]

According to Locke and Newton the reason that the cup looks the particular colour it does to me is determined by the properties of the cup-gap. For example, Locke claimed that: "what is Sweet, Blue, or Warm in *Idea*, is but the certain Bulk, Figure, and Motion of the insensible Parts in the Bodies themselves, which we call so".[5] However, other

---

[4] Isaac Newton, *Opticks, Or a Treatise of the Reflections, Refractions, Inflections and Colours of Light,* New York: Dover Publications, 1730/1952, pp. 124-5.

[5] John Locke, *An Essay Concerning Human Understanding,* ed. P. H. Nidditch, Oxford: Oxford University Press, (1690/1975), %15.

dispositionalists deny that the particular colour that I perceive is due to the properties of the cup-gap. One such philosopher is C. L. Hardin.

Hardin argues that there are a plethora of physical properties of objects which influence their perceived colour and that therefore: "it would be in vain to suppose that objects sharing a common color resemble one another in physical structure."[6] Furthermore, Hardin rejects the idea that there could be a family of diverse physical structures which share a disposition to radiate light of a particular character from their surfaces. This is because, "it is unlikely that any two things chosen at

---

[6] C. L. Hardin, *Color for Philosophers*, Cambridge: Hackett Publishing Company, 1988, p. 4.

random which look to have the same blue color under normal conditions will have identical reflection spectra, let alone identical spectra of the other sorts."[7] These considerations cause Hardin to conclude that colours cannot be located in the cup-gap: "We are to be eliminativists with respect to colour as a property of objects"[8]; but contra-Locke and contra-Newton, they also cause Hardin to conclude that the particular colours which I perceive are determined by properties within me: "At the present moment there isn't the slightest reason to

---

[7] C. L. Hardin, *Color for Philosophers*, Cambridge: Hackett Publishing Company, 1988, p. 7.

[8] C. L. Hardin, *Color for Philosophers*, Cambridge: Hackett Publishing Company, 1988, p. 112.

think that there is a set of external physical properties that is the analog of the fourfold structure of the colors that we experience"[9]. According to this view a *complete* analysis of the properties of the cup-gap at t_1 would *not* reveal which colour I perceive.

So, whilst there are two variants of dispositionalism, *all* dispositionalists hold that at t_2 the cup-gap is wholly devoid of colour; all it contains is the disposition to appear coloured if perceived.

---

[9] C. L. Hardin, *Color for Philosophers*, Cambridge: Hackett Publishing Company, 1988, p. xxi.

Chapter 2

At t_2 the cup-gap was coloured the same colour as the colour which I perceived at t_1 and t_3 (green)

Our second possibility is that at t_2 the cup-gap is coloured and that it is coloured *solely* the colour that it appears to me to be at t_1 and t_3. So, according to this view the cup-gap is literally coloured green at t_1, t_2 and t_3 it is just that at t_2 I am unable to perceive that the cup-gap is green. Let us refer to this view as the 'Intrinsic Property' view. This view of colour was prevalent two thousand years ago:

> the ancient Greeks...regard[ed] colour as an intrinsic property, requiring light only to activate it like electricity activating a lightbulb.[10]

There are two groups of contemporary philosophers who claim that the colour green can be identified with properties of the cup-gap – the 'objectivist physicalists' and the 'primitivists'. The 'objectivist physicalists' assert that colours are identical to physical properties. So, J. J. C. Smart claims that: "colours are physical properties of the

---

[10] Philip Ball, *Bright Earth: The Invention of Colour*, London: Vintage, 2008, p. 39.

surfaces of objects."[11] Whilst, D. M. Armstrong claims that:

> The particular primary qualities with which Smart, Lewis and myself propose to identify the secondary qualities will fairly clearly be *structural* properties at the microscopic level...if we can find a physical property which qualifies red things (what a good theory will tell us are red things) and bestows the same powers as the powers of red things, including their powers to act on us, then it

---

[11] J. J. C. Smart, "Reply to Armstrong" in *Readings on Color: The Philosophy of Color*, Volume 1, Ed. Alex Byrne and David R. Hilbert, London: MIT Press, 2001, p. 47.

will be a good bet that this property *is* redness.[12]

In contrast, the 'primitivists' assert that colours are not identical to physical properties because they are *sui generis*. For example, John Campbell argues that colours supervene on physical properties:

> On this view, redness, for example, is not a disposition to produce experiences in us. It is, rather, the ground of such a disposition. But that is not because redness is a microphysical

---

[12] D. M. Armstrong, "Smart and the Secondary Qualities" in *Readings on Color: The Philosophy of Color*, Volume 1, Ed. Alex Byrne and David R. Hilbert, London: MIT Press, 2001, pp. 42-3.

property – the real nature of the property is, rather, transparent to us... colours are supervenient upon physical properties, if only in the minimal sense that two possible worlds which share all their physical characteristics cannot be differently coloured.[13]

Campbell stresses that an 'objective' description of the world can be one in which mind-independent properties – such as colours – are absent; he sees the failure to understand this fact as the central objection which is raised against the primitivist. On

---

[13] John Campbell, "A Simple View of Colour" in *Readings on Color: The Philosophy of Color*, Volume 1, Ed. Alex Byrne and David R. Hilbert, London: MIT Press, 2001, p. 178.

The Nature of Colour

this account, as colours supervene on physical properties, the cup-gap at t_2 will be solely coloured green; this means that there is no possibility of colour spectrum inversion:

> the qualitative character of a colour-experience is inherited from the qualitative character of the colour. It depends on which colour-tracking capacity is being exercised in having the experience. So if you and I are tracking the same colours, our colour-experiences are qualitatively identical. This

view does not allow for the hypothesis of spectrum inversion[14]

Whilst the 'objective physicalists' and the 'primitivists' argue that *colours can be identified with properties of the cup-gap* it needs to be noted that some of them actually seem to sometimes use the word 'colour' to refer to parts of the world which they conceive to be wholly devoid of colour! Of course, if one claims that properties of the cup-gap can be identified with 'colours' but *uses the word*

---

[14] John Campbell, "A Simple View of Colour" in *Readings on Color: The Philosophy of Color*, Volume 1, Ed. Alex Byrne and David R. Hilbert, London: MIT Press, 2001, p. 189.

'colours' not to refer to colours then one is actually a 'Dispositionalist' about colour.

So, according to the Intrinsic Property view at t_2 the cup-gap *is* coloured and it is solely coloured green.

Chapter 3

At t_2 the cup-gap was coloured a particular but different colour to the colour which I perceived at t_1 and t_3

Let us now consider the odd-sounding possibility that at t_2 the cup-gap was a particular colour but that this colour was a different colour to the colour which I perceived at t_1 and t_3 (green). On this view at t_2 the cup-gap could have been coloured 'red', or it could have been coloured a colour which humans are unable to perceive and therefore have no name for.

The Nature of Colour

In this view not only is the cup-gap at t_2 a completely different colour to the colour which I perceived at t_1 and t_3, but it is also the case that at t_1 and t_3 the cup-gap is a completely different colour to the colour that I perceive at t_1 and t_3.

An account of this kind has seemingly been recently defended by Peter Unger. Unger's motivation for his account is his disagreement with Locke:

> Locke didn't allow that basic physical reality should have any Qualitative Color... we should liberate ourselves from the Denial, as stultifying as it's unnecessary.[15]

---

[15] Peter Unger, *All the Power in the World*, Oxford: Oxford University Press, 2006, p. 168.

A Particular but Different Colour

From this starting point Unger develops an account in which all parts of physical reality have definite colours but in which perceivers are unable to perceive what these colours are. So:

> In this actual world, and in this present Eon of the world, it seems quite certain, at least to me, that there aren't any sentient beings able to perceive how it is Qualitatively with a Spatially Extensibly Qualitied physical object... For example, even if it should be that, in our World and in our Eon, every electron is the very same Absolutely Specific Shade of Extensible Color, say Transparent Blue, there won't be any perceivers, in our World, and in

our Eon, who're ever able to perceive any of the electrons to be (Transparent) Blue.[16]

It is clearly possible that there are two very different types of colours, those that are located in the unperceived world and those which a perceiver perceives when they perceive the world. Unger seems to believe that it is possible that the 'basic concreta' of the world could be coloured a colour that a human cannot experience – they could be coloured 'Lorly' – but when a human perceives an object that is in actuality coloured 'Lorly' they perceive the very different colour 'Red':

---

[16] Peter Unger, *All the Power in the World*, Oxford: Oxford University Press, 2006, p. 112.

A Particular but Different Colour

Supposing that our hypothesis is right…it's likely that actual physical things *won't* be Spatially Extensibly Colored in any of the Absolute Specific Ways that, quite directly and clearly, *we can conceive them to be Colored*… But, still, the basic concreta, in our actual world, will be Extensibly Spatially Colored concreta. Their space will be pervaded by less available Absolutely Specific Color Qualities… Let's call one them Col, another Lor. So, though it may be that no real spatial concreta are Qualitied Redly, many may be Qualitied Lorly.[17]

---

[17] Peter Unger, *All the Power in the World*, Oxford: Oxford University Press, 2006, p. 168.

So, according to the view outlined in this chapter – a view which I will call the 'We-know-not-what' view – at t_2 (and t_1 and t_3) the cup-gap is coloured a particular colour we-know-not-what, it would perhaps be coloured 'Lorly'.

Chapter 4

At t_2 the cup-gap was coloured but it wasn't a particular colour

Finally, let us consider the possibility that at t_2 the cup-gap wasn't wholly devoid of colour but that it also wasn't a particular colour. In other words, the cup-gap was a plethora of intermingling colours. This account entails that the unperceived world is not determinately coloured but that every point in the world contains a plethora of colours. So, according to this view, whilst a perceiver can only perceive one colour in a particular location at any given time, the world actually contains a multitude of colours at this location.

According to this view the colour that I perceive at t_1 and t_3 is located in the cup-gap. There are two different accounts which seek to explain why I perceive green in the cup-gap when the cup-gap actually contains a plethora of colours. According to the first account it is properties in the cup-gap which determine that I perceive green. So, Aristotle argues that:

> for when light falls on something, and, being tinted by it, becomes reddish or greenish, and then the reflected light falls on another colour, being again mixed by it, it takes on still

another mixture of colour. And being affected in this way, continually but imperceptibly, it sometimes reaches the eyes as a mixture of many colours, but producing the sensation of the most predominant[18]

According to the second account it is the structure of my visual perceptual apparatus which causes me to perceive the cup-gap as green rather than as the intricate interfusion of a plethora of colours that the cup-gap actually is. On this account the green that I perceive is located in the cup-gap, whilst my visual perceptual apparatus operates as a filtering

---

[18] Aristotle, 'On Colours', *Aristotle: Minor Works*, Trans. W. S. Hett, London: William Heinemann Ltd, pp. 17-19.

device which has no access to the non-green colours in the cup-gap. On this view, as it is the structure of my visual perceptual apparatus which determines which colours I perceive, it follows that if instead of me perceiving the cup-gap at t_1 a different perceiver took my place that that perceiver could perceive a non-green colour. As most humans have very similar visual perceptual structures one would expect that most humans would perceive the same colour. However, it is clearly more likely that an entity with a very different visual perceptual structure would perceive a non-green colour when they perceive the cup.

This account of colour is concordant with the views of physicist Frank Wilczek who philosopher

Evan Thompson claims is "a leading physicist"[19]. According to Wilczek:

> Science early discovered that light "in itself" has a much richer structure than our sense of vision reveals. It therefore becomes necessary to distinguish <u>physical colour</u> from <u>sensory colour</u>. It is possible to predict the sensation people will report when a given bundle of light rays impinges on their eyes – that is, the sensory colour – in terms of the physical colours present in the rays. On the other hand, there are combinations of light that are defi-

---

[19] Evan Thompson, *Colour Vision*, London: Routledge, 1995, p. 16.

The Nature of Colour

nitely different but look the same. Physical colour is, in this precise sense, more fundamental than sensory colour, even though the latter is what we actually see.[20]

as far as we know there is a continuous infinity of possible pure colours. Some light is refracted through each of a continuum of slightly different angles emerging from the prism, and the light at each angle represents a different pure colour.[21]

---

[20] Frank Wilczek and Betsy Devine, *Longing for the Harmonies: Themes and Variations from Modern Physics*, London: W. M. Norton & Company, 1988, p. 6.

[21] Frank Wilczek and Betsy Devine, *Longing for the Harmonies: Themes and Variations from Modern Physics*, London: W. M. Norton & Company, 1988, p. 9.

Coloured but not a Particular Colour

So, as the complete range of sensory colours that a human can perceive arises from different combinations of only three pure colours, whilst the world itself contains a "continuous infinity of possible pure colours", it follows that the world itself is truly an intermingling web of a multitude of colours only a few of which any one perceiver can possibly ever perceive. In Wilczek's words: "we are all colour blind. At best, we perceive three averages from an infinite manifold of physical colours."[22]

---

[22] Frank Wilczek and Betsy Devine, *Longing for the Harmonies: Themes and Variations from Modern Physics*, London: W. M. Norton & Company, 1988, p. 10.

The Nature of Colour

So, whilst there are two variants of the 'Infinite Manifold' view, *all* advocates of this view assert that at t_2 (and t_1 and t_3) the cup-gap contains a multitude of colours of which green is just one.

Chapter 5

Summary

We have considered four possible answers to the following question:

At t_2 was the cup-gap coloured or was it wholly devoid of colour?

Answer 1   Dispositionalism

According to this view the cup-gap is wholly devoid of colour, and the colour that I perceive (green) is either created by non-coloured properties of the cup-gap (Locke/Newton) or by non-coloured properties of my perceptual apparatus (Hardin). On either possibility the green that I perceive is located 'in me' and not in the cup-gap (assuming that greenness doesn't shoot out of my eyes into the cup-gap when I perceive the cup-gap).

Answer 2   The Intrinsic Property View

According to this view the cup-gap is coloured solely green because green is an intrinsic property of the cup-gap which exists in the absence of a perceiver.

Summary

On this view the green that I perceive is located in the cup-gap and not in me.

Answer 3   The 'We-know-not-what' View

According to this view the cup-gap is coloured a particular colour we-know-not-what (such as 'Lorly' or 'red'). This means that on this view the colour 'we-know-not-what' is located in the cup-gap, whilst the colour green is located in me.

The Nature of Colour

Answer 4   The Infinite Manifold View

According to this view the cup-gap contains a multitude of colours of which green is just one. On this view the colour green that I perceive is located in the cup-gap and not in me.

Chapter 6

Reasons to favour the 'Infinite Manifold' view

Reason 1

The Intrinsic Property view is too simplistic because there is a compelling scientific account according to which the colour a perceiver perceives is dependent upon the structure of the perceptual apparatus of the perceiver. It is this scientific account which caused Hardin to deny that a complete analysis of the physical properties of the cup-gap could reveal the fact that I am perceiving green.

The Nature of Colour

Reason 2

The 'We-know-not-what' account is too extravagant. If the cup-gap appears to me to be green then to *both* deny that there is green in the cup-gap *and* to assert that the cup-gap is actually coloured a different colour such as 'Lorly' is hard to accept (it is much more plausible to assert that *if* there is colour in the cup-gap *then* green is in the cup-gap).

Reasons to favour the 'IM' view

Reason 3

Agreement with Unger's objection to Dispositionalism that the denial of colours to the unperceived world is "stultifying" and "unnecessary".

Furthermore, Secondary Qualities are not separable from Primary Qualities.

The Nature of Colour

Reason 4

The Infinite Manifold view has the advantages of:

A) Not denying that the unperceived world is wholly devoid of colour

B) Not denying that the cup-gap is wholly devoid of green

C) Advocating an active role for the perceiver in determining which colour is perceived (in the second version of the view)

www.ingramcontent.com/pod-product-compliance
Lightning Source LLC
Chambersburg PA
CBHW061300040426
42444CB00010B/2440